NWH

A Robbie Reader

A Robbie Reader

The Ancient Mystery of Easter Island

John A. Torres

Mitchell Lane
PUBLISHERS

P.O. Box 196
Hockessin, Delaware 19707
Visit us on the web: www.mitchelllane.com
Comments? email us:
mitchelllane@mitchelllane.com

Mitchell Lane PUBLISHERS

Copyright © 2007 by Mitchell Lane Publishers. All rights reserved. No part of this book may be reproduced without written permission from the publisher. Printed and bound in the United States of America.

Printing   1   2   3   4   5   6   7   8   9

A Robbie Reader/Natural Disasters

The Ancient Mystery of Easter Island
The Bermuda Triangle
Bubonic Plague
Earthquake in Loma Prieta, California, 1989
The Fury of Hurricane Andrew, 1992
Hurricane Katrina, 2005
The Lost Continent of Atlantis
Mt. Vesuvius and the Destruction of Pompeii, A.D. 79
Mudslide in La Conchita, California, 2005
Tsunami Disaster in Indonesia, 2004
Where Did All the Dinosaurs Go?

Library of Congress Cataloging-in-Publication Data
Torres, John Albert.
    The ancient mystery of Easter Island / by John Torres.
        p. cm. — (A Robbie reader. Natural disasters)
    Includes bibliographical references and index.
    ISBN 1-58415-495-0 (library bound)
    1. Easter Island—History—Juvenile literature. 2. Easter Island—Antiquities—
Juvenile literature. I. Title. II. Series.
    F3169.T67 2007
    996.1' 8—dc22
                                                                    2006006104

ISBN-10: 1-58415-495-0   ISBN-13: 9781584154952

ABOUT THE AUTHOR: John A. Torres is an award-winning journalist who covers social issues for *Florida Today*. John has also written more than 40 books for various publishers on a variety of topics, including *P. Diddy*; *Clay Aiken*; *Disaster in the Indian Ocean, Tsunami, 2004*; and *Hurricane Katrina and the Devastation of New Orleans, 2005* for Mitchell Lane Publishers. In his spare time, John likes playing sports, going to theme parks, and fishing with his children, stepchildren, and wife, Jennifer.

PHOTO CREDITS: Cover, p. 1—Martin Bernetti/AFP/Getty Images; p. 4—Bjarte Sorensen; p. 7—Aurbina; pp. 8, 17—Thor Heyerdahl; pp. 10, 24—Sharon Beck; p. 13—Roger Viollet/Getty Images; pp. 13, 18, 21, 27—Age Fotostock/Superstock; p. 23—Duncan Wright.

PUBLISHER'S NOTE: The following story has been thoroughly researched and to the best of our knowledge represents a true story. While every possible effort has been made to ensure accuracy, the publisher will not assume liability for damages caused by inaccuracies in the data, and makes no warranty on the accuracy of the information contained herein.
    To reflect current usage, we have chosen to use the secular era designations BCE ("before the common era") and CE ("of the common era") instead of the traditional designations BC ("before Christ") and AD (*anno Domini*, "in the year of the Lord").
                                                                    PLB

TABLE OF CONTENTS

Words in **bold** type can be found in the glossary.

One of the giant statues found on Easter Island was erected on Ahu Tahai. American archaeologist William Mulloy restored the statue's coral eyes.

An Island of Secrets

No one knew why the powerful Uoke did not like islands. And no one could stop this gigantic god from doing what he liked to do best. Uoke would go to an island, stick his huge lever underneath it, and fling it into the sea. There, the island would sink.

When Uoke got to one particular island in the Pacific Ocean, his lever broke in the island's hard **volcanic** rock. He was unable to sink it, and the land that would later be known as Easter Island was saved.

The story of Uoke is only one of many **legends** associated with this tiny island, which is steeped in mystery and tragedy. Easter Island is filled with unknowns: Where did the people originally come from? What happened to all the trees? Did the people really eat one another? Most curiously, how did they build the hundreds of 30-foot-high stone statues that dot the landscape?

The stone giants, called **moai**, solemnly keep watch over the land. Many have large strong foreheads, a long nose and jaws, and extended ears. Some are on the coast and others are miles inland. Some are standing on stone platforms, called **ahu**, and others have fallen down. Some statues are wearing headdresses made of red stone, and others have large pieces of coral for eyes.

Archaeologists (ar-kee-AH-luh-jists) and **engineering** (en-jeh-NEER-ring) experts over the last few hundred years have debated and tried to guess how these enormous stone structures were built and moved. Just as mysterious is why the people stopped making them. A few dozen statues remain on the island uncompleted, even though thousands of stonecutting tools were left scattered about.

Moai on the slope of Rano Raraku face the sea from Easter Island. Are they supposed to be looking at something in particular? Notice the shape of the chins and the length of the ears. Some people believe these are clues as to who built these giant wonders.

These archaeologists and students use a knotted rope to measure the height of this statue. The head is about 20 feet tall. However, part of the statue may be buried.

All but a handful of the statues built on Easter Island are made up of compressed ash from the volcanoes—rock that is especially good for carving. No one can explain why the work stopped so abruptly, with many statues left unfinished. Was there a war between neighboring tribes? Did a disease spring up and kill the strongest workers? Was there an earthquake? If so, would these superstitious people have believed that one of their angry gods had sent the quake, so they stopped building?

To try to understand the mysteries of Easter Island, it is important to understand where it lies and what types of people lived there.

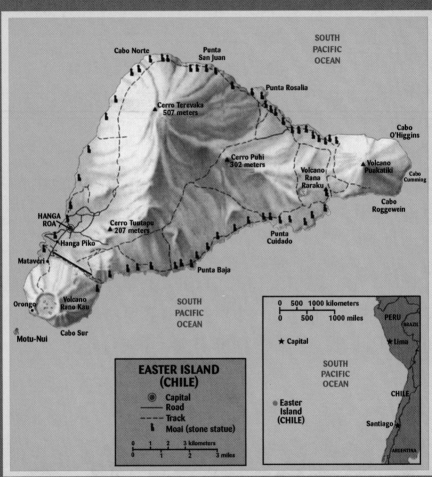

Easter Island, a land of volcanoes, lies about 2,000 miles from Chile. The moai were carved from the extinct volcano Rano Raraku, and many of them were placed around the coast. The capital city of Hanga Roa boasts an airport and several hotels.

The Middle of the Ocean

Easter Island is one of the **remotest** places in the world. The **triangular** piece of volcanic rock is about 14 miles long and 7 miles wide. It sits in the Pacific Ocean directly between the Polynesian country of Tahiti and the South American country of Chile. The island was once known as *Te Pito o Te Henúa,* or the Navel of the World. Now it is also called Rapa Nui, as are its native peoples.

There is an old, **extinct** volcano in each corner of the island, and the landscape changes from place to place. There are lush, rolling green hills. Volcanic eruptions from thousands of years ago have created harsh craters in the land. Very steep and sudden cliffs plunge straight down toward the ocean. There are trees there now, but at one time, there were none.

There is some debate as to who the first inhabitants of the island were. Evidence from ancient bones suggests that tribes of **Polynesians** may have been among the first to find the island. They traveled to it over and over from across the ocean. That an ancient people could repeatedly find this tiny piece of rock indicates they were skilled **navigators**.

"The chances of Easter Island being reached even once are extremely limited; to imagine it being reached several times over vast distances is beyond belief," write historians John Flenley and Paul Bahn.

Archaeologists believe that Polynesian **migrants** settled on the island between 400 and 800 CE. They started carving the massive statues, but no one today is really sure why. They may have built them to honor ancestors or to honor one or more of their gods. They

The crater of Rano Kau is on the western point of Easter Island. Archaeologists believe the statues on the island were created by carving rock that was found in the crater of Rano Raraku, which makes up the eastern point.

probably moved them using a system of rolling logs. It is believed they mastered the skill of sculpting statues and lived peaceful lives for eight hundred years or more.

If so, what went wrong on Easter Island?

By the time famous British explorer Captain James Cook found Easter Island, it was in ruins and the people were suffering from hunger and poverty.

The End of an Era

Some scientists believe that the small island became **overpopulated** and people began to separate into different tribes. Because too many people were living on the island, resources became scarce. Forests were gone from the island. They had been cut down to help move the moai and for firewood. Soon people began fighting over choice lands. That is probably when the problems began.

There is evidence that palms and other kinds of trees once grew on the island. When the trees were gone, the soil in which crops could grow was washed into the sea. Without wood to make or repair their fishing boats, and without crops to eat, the people began to starve. They may have had to resort to **cannibalism** to survive.

Some accounts say that "long-eared people" fought the "short-eared people," and that the winners would tear down their enemies' statues. This story would explain why so many statues lay scattered as if knocked down by a giant. The winning tribes, the story says, would eat the losers.

In 1722, a group of Dutch explorers found the island. They became the first **Europeans** to set foot on the rocky soil. Because it was Easter Sunday, Admiral Jacob Roggeveen named it Easter Island.

The explorers spent only one day on the island. They wrote about wild natives dancing around huge fires and worshiping stone statues. There was an argument between the Dutch and some of the natives. The Dutch, with rifles to their advantage, shot and killed at least 12 natives before leaving.

About 50 years later, in 1770, a group of Spanish explorers from the colony of Peru

Easter Island natives seem to have been influenced by Polynesia and South America. They perform a Grunting Pig Dance, a traditional dance from Polynesia.

claimed the island as belonging to the kingdom of Spain. A few years after that, famous British seafarer James Cook found the island as well.

When Cook landed on the island, it was in ruins. Its people were suffering from great poverty and hunger. Most of the statues had been toppled, but the history of what the people had accomplished was still amazing. Some of these creations weighed as much as 80,000 pounds—and had been carried miles and miles inland.

Motu-Nui is an islet off the coast of Easter Island. Every year a member from each clan would swim across to Motu-Nui in search of the first egg left by the sooty tern (an island bird). The winner would be in charge of natural resources for the next year. Birdmen are carved in the rocks in the foreground.

The Statues

The mystery of what happened on Easter Island may lie with the giant statues of big-jawed, long-eared creatures that exist only in stone. It took groves of forests to be able to roll the statues from their volcanic quarry at Ranu Raraku to the inland ahu.

Killing the forests to help move the statues had a lasting impact on the land. The Polynesian rat was introduced on the island when the first migrants arrived, and they feasted on seeds of the trees. No new trees could grow. Birdlife eventually died out because there were no trees in which the birds could make their nests. And with the disappearance of the forests, no more boats could be built. The people could no longer fish for food. Some historians say that this is when the natives turned to cannibalism—eating one another for food when the natural resources dwindled.

Whether that is true or not remains to be seen. It is known that the inhabitants of Easter Island also feasted on sweet potatoes—their main crop—as well as on gourds. These probably came from the South American explorers representing Spain.

When they weren't harvesting these crops, they were making statues. Not all of the statues were of humans or creatures resembling humans. They also carved masks, birds, birdmen, turtles, monsters, and other strange creatures.

Carvings done on rocks are known as **petroglyphs**. Individual glyphs represent part of an idea or word.

While the native peoples did not use an alphabet like we have to communicate, the people used their own version, called

The written language of Easter Island was Rongorongo. Each detailed symbol is less than half an inch high (the symbols above have been enlarged). No one in modern times has been able to translate the mysterious writing.

Rongorongo, as their script. The characters were mainly picture symbols that were used to express ideas as well as objects.

Besides the loss of the forest, other events worked to destroy the island's people. Whalers stopping on the island would leave behind deadly diseases. In the mid-1800s, traders from Peru raided the island, taking 1,500 of the strongest natives to sell as slaves. In the 1860s, a smallpox **epidemic** killed nearly

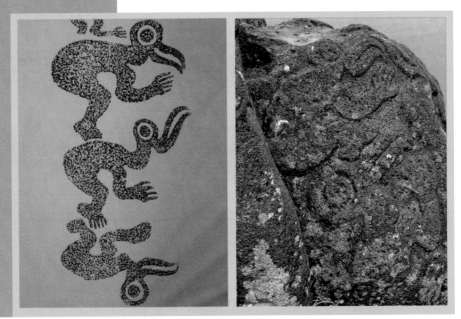

Petroglyphs are symbols carved on rock. The birdmen petroglyphs were carved when the competition to determine the island's leader involved bringing a bird's egg from Motu-Nui.

everyone on the island. Only about 110 people remained to rebuild and repopulate.

The population that survived had to be very careful with their remaining natural resources. They had to ration their supplies. Soon a competition was developed that would determine which clan member would be in charge of allocating resources for the coming year.

The sooty tern was important to the culture of Easter Island. The first islander to find a tern egg would be in charge of the island's resources for the next year.

One representative of each clan would dive into the ocean and swim across to Motu-Nui, a nearby tiny island. This is where an ocean bird known as the sooty tern would nest. Whichever swimmer came back first with a tern egg would be the winner of the competition and find himself in charge for the next year. It was a sacred but lonely task. The leader would sit inside all day in the shade. He could talk to no one but his special servants.

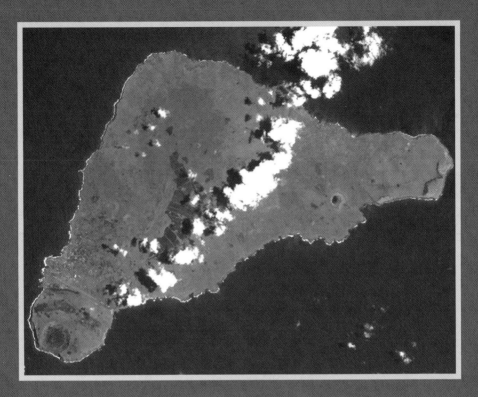

Volcanic eruptions have left giant scars on the surface of Easter Island. Some of these craters are filled with water.

A Modern View

There will always be some who believe that the answers to the mysteries of Easter Island lie in outer space with extraterrestrials or shrouded in magic and sorcery. But for most scientists and archaeologists, a lot of the mystery is gone.

Most experts now agree that the statues must have been created on the island out of volcanic rock and moved by rolling them along on giant logs. The resulting deforestation—the cutting down of forests—is also what ultimately led to the society's downfall. The environment could no longer sustain so many people.

Some believe the loss of the forests also explains why many statues were left incomplete, with tools still sitting beside the unfinished work. Dying of starvation, the people became angry with their gods. They stopped creating these giant tributes to them. After a while, they stopped talking about the statues, and the history of how they came to be made was lost.

Since 1888, Rapa Nui has belonged to Chile, a South American country about 2,000 miles away. Daily flights from Chile and Tahiti service the tourist trade. They also take native Easter Islanders to the mainland, where many have attended college. Some who find jobs there will stay on the mainland for years at a time.

By 2006, less than 4,000 islanders lived on the tiny piece of rock in the middle of the ocean. To them, the incredible statues that dot the island are part of everyday life. To the 15,000 tourists who come every year, the island's mysteries are fascinating.

The island survives with the money brought in by these tourists. The thriving tourist industry is made up of archaeology students, mystery lovers, and those who just want to see

The moai at Hanga Roa were arranged to look inland. Archaeologists believe they were set up to watch over a village that thrived there hundreds of years ago.

the magnificent statues and explore Easter Island—a sort of open-air museum.

One popular legend that tourists learn tells of an old man who could not speak and who appeared mysteriously on the island. He motioned with his hands that he was tired and hungry. He was given a place to sleep, but no one brought him food. He became angry. At one point during the night, the old man tapped his feet loudly against the sides of the house, causing a great noise. With that, the statues fell over and they were never built again.

27

CHRONOLOGY

5500 BCE   People in Melanesia voyage in boats near Easter Island. It is possible they found it.

400s CE*   Polynesian sailors begin to settle on the island.

1000   Population of Easter Island starts to grow significantly.

1100   People on Easter Island begin carving huge statues from volcanic rock.

1300s   The population starts to decline as trees begin to vanish.

1600s   Cannibalism begins on Easter Island. Statue building is halted.

1722   Dutch explorers led by Admiral Jacob Roggeveen land on the island and name it Easter Island. There are no trees there.

1774   Captain James Cook lands on the island.

1860s   Slave traders from Peru raid the island.

1877   Only 110 islanders remain after a smallpox epidemic.

1888   The island is claimed by Chile.

1966   Chile declares the island a province.

1976   A small hospital is built on the island.

1986   NASA expands landing strip on Easter Island for possible space shuttle emergency landing.

2002   The island's population is 3,791.

2006   Tourism is the main industry, with 15,000 people visiting the island every year. There is talk of building cell phone towers on the island.

*No one knows for sure. Some sources claim that sailors arrived 700–800 CE.

TIMELINE IN HISTORY

1000   Norwegian Leif Eriksson explores the east coast of North America.

1215   The Magna Carta is signed in England, proclaiming basic rights for all people.

1492   Christopher Columbus stumbles upon America.

1513   Ponce de León lands in Florida.

1609   Henry Hudson explores North America and what will be the Hudson River.

1770s   Smallpox claims one third of Native Americans living in the Pacific Northwest.

1779   On his third voyage around the world, Captain James Cook is killed in Hawaii.

1835   Charles Darwin studies the wildlife on remote Galápagos Island. He begins forming his theory of evolution.

1911   Raold Amundsen leads an expedition to the South Pole.

1920s   Mysterious Nazca lines are discovered in Peru.

1969   Humans venture to the moon in their quest to explore space.

2006   Scientists discover IOK-1, a galaxy they estimate to be 13 billion light-years away.

FIND OUT MORE

Books

Routledge, Katherine. *The Mystery of Easter Island.* New York: Cosimo Books, 2005.

Orliac, Catherine, and Michel Orliac. *Easter Island: Mystery of the Stone Giants.* New York: Henry N. Abrams, 1995.

Works Consulted

BBC. "The Mystery of Easter Island." Narrated by John Shrapnel. January 9, 2003.
http://www.bbc.co.uk/science/horizon/2003/ easterislandtrans.shtml

Easter Island Foundation: http://www.islandheritage.org/ index.html

Flenley, John, and Paul Bahn. *The Enigmas of Easter Island.* London: Oxford University Press, 2002.

Heyerdahl, Thor. *Aku-Aku: The Secret of Easter Island.* Chicago: Rand McNally & Co., 1958.

Maziere, Francis. *Mysteries of Easter Island.* London: Collins Books, 1969.

Pratt, David. "Easter Island: Land of Mystery," November 2004.
http://ourworld.compuserve.com/homepages/dp5/ easter1.htm#e1

On the Internet

Clark, Liesl. "First Inhabitants." *NOVA,* November 2000.
http://www.pbs.org/wgbh/nova/easter/civilization/ first.html

Easter Island Foundation.
http://www.islandheritage.org/index.html

Mysterious Places: Easter Island.
http://www.mysteriousplaces.com/Easter_Island/ index.html

Mystic Places: Easter Island. Discovery Channel.
http://www.exn.ca/mysticplaces/easterisland.asp

GLOSSARY

ahu (AH-hoo)–One of the stone pedestals on which the statues on Easter Island were placed.

archaeologists (ar-kee-AH-luh-jists)–People who study past human civilizations.

cannibalism (KAA-nih-bah-lism)–The practice of human beings eating other human beings.

engineering (en-jeh-NEER-ring)–The science of making useful things.

epidemic (eh-peh-DEH-mik)–An outbreak of a disease that affects a large segment of the population.

Europeans (yur-uh-PEE-uns)–The people who live in or come from the continent of Europe. Some countries in Europe include England, Italy, France, and Germany.

extinct (ek-STINKT)–To no longer be active; to have completely died out.

legend (LEH-jund)–A popular myth or story that is passed down from one generation to the next.

migrants (MY-grints)–People who move from one place to another in order to find work or food.

moai (MOH-ay)–The ancient giant statues that dot Easter Island.

navigators (NAA-vih-GAY-turs)–People who figure out routes from one place to another.

overpopulated (oh-ver-PAH-pyoo-lay-ted)–Having so many of one species living in a certain area that the individuals have trouble surviving.

petroglyph (PEH-troh-glif)–A carving or inscription on a rock.

Polynesians (pah-lih-NEE-zhuns)–People who come from or live on the islands of Polynesia in the South Pacific.

remotest (reh-MOH-tist)–The most out-of-the-way place.

triangular (try-ANG-yoo-ler)–Something that is shaped like a triangle.

volcanic (vol-KAA-nik)–Produced by a volcano, such as rock or ash.

INDEX